Cultural Competence

A Guide for Human Service Agencies
(REVISED)

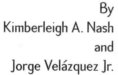

By
Kimberleigh A. Nash
and
Jorge Velázquez Jr.

CWLA Press · Washington, DC

CWLA Press is an imprint of the Child Welfare League of America. The Child Welfare League of America (CWLA), the nation's oldest and largest membership-based child welfare organization, is committed to engaging all Americans in promoting the well-being of children and protecting every child from harm.

CHILD WELFARE LEAGUE OF AMERICA, INC.

440 First Street, NW, Third Floor, Washington, DC 20001-2085

E-mail: books@cwla.org

CURRENT PRINTING (last digit)

10 9 8 7 6 5 4 3 2 1

Cover design by Mary Flannery/Jennifer Geanakos

Printed in the United States of America

ISBN # 0-87868-871-4

Contents

Acknowledgements

The Child Welfare League of America (CWLA) thanks everyone who contributed to the *Advancing Cultural Competence in Child Welfare Initiative,* sponsored by The Prudential Foundation. Through this initiative, CWLA expanded its capacity to assist the child welfare field in providing services and supports to children and families that are relevant to their cultural values and appropriate to their needs.

CWLA is indebted to The Prudential Foundation for its funding and support, which enabled the research necessary for this guide. CWLA thanks the foundation for its continued support of issues that affect the health and well-being of children and families.

In addition, CWLA thanks the advisory committee, which worked diligently to produce consultation pieces for executive leadership and management teams (to which this guide is a companion). This committee enthusiastically provided their experience and expertise, which enriched this book. Special thanks to Sheryl Brissett-Chapman, Nancy E. Cavaluzzi, Frances C. Frazier, Regis G. McDonald, Jean Tucker Mann, Dianne Bostic Robinson, and Layla P. Suleiman.

Dana Burdnell Wilson, Director of CWLA's Mid-Atlantic Region and former Program Director for cultural competence, set the tone and mapped the course for this project from its inception. Her tireless efforts and continued support are greatly appreciated.

Introduction

In its 1988–1990 Strategic Plan, CWLA's Board of Directors included a goal to address the "ethnic and cultural diversity of all the children in the child welfare system." CWLA decided to make cultural competence part of its commitment to children and families. As part of that commitment, with support from The Prudential Foundation, CWLA published *Cultural Competence: A Guide for Human Service Agencies*.

Today, the challenges CWLA member agencies and other child welfare service providers face are more complex than ever. Communities are more demographically diverse and dynamic, as a result of increased immigration, refugee resettlement, and the increased mobility of families (U.S. Bureau of the Census, 2001). These dynamics and increased diversity are challenging child welfare agencies and practitioners to develop a greater understanding of more complex communities.

In addition, economic, social, ethnic, racial, spiritual, and other cultural factors influence the number of challenges faced by children and families. Census 2000 showed the United States to be more ethnically and racially diverse than at any other time in its history. This must be considered and incorporated into the strategic plans and implementation processes of any agency that provides services to culturally diverse communities.

These social changes, coupled with the demands of a more outcome-driven environment, a punitive outlook by society of families in the child welfare system, anti-immigration sentiment, and socioeconomic conditions, challenge today's leaders. Given the range of pressures that affect agencies, child welfare executives face the dilemma of whether to focus on cultural competence as an organizational goal.

Children of color are disproportionately represented in the child welfare system, particularly in out-of-home care and the juvenile justice system. (Children of color in child welfare are ethnically diverse and primarily include those of Latino, African American, Asian American, and Native American cultures.) Children of color remain in these systems for longer periods of time and are less likely to be reunited with their families than children of European descent.

Poverty is a common characteristic among children and families served in child welfare. The ramifications of poverty—unemployment, inadequate education, inferior or nonexistent health care, substandard housing, and welfare dependence—all increase the likelihood that children in poor families will need the services of the child welfare system at some point.

The diverse cultures served by the child welfare system should raise questions about which policies, programs, and practices are appropriate to a child's and family's cultural values, traditions, needs, and expectations. This issue challenges the child welfare system to extend itself in support of the premise that effective child welfare practices are directly related to the knowledge and understanding of, as well as sensitivity and responsiveness to, the culture of the client population. This issue, as well as the task of recruiting and retaining a qualified diverse staff, present not only challenges, but also opportunities for more effective leadership, management, and service delivery.

Child welfare agencies respond to issues of cultural competence in different ways. Many child welfare agencies aggressively shape organizational agendas that encompass a broad vision; expanded goals and objectives; and modified policies, procedures, and programs to better meet families' needs. The management teams of these organizations are attempting to raise their individual comfort levels by gaining an understanding of their own cultural backgrounds and biases, the cultures of others, and multicultural organizational behavior. They are learning how to positively manage culture in their organizations—and learning how to integrate and enjoy the benefits of cultural diversity.

The one-size-fits-all approach denies the pluralistic society of America, the changing face of child welfare, and the resulting cultural diversity that is an inevitable part of day-to-day experience.

CWLA developed this guide to provide child welfare and social service organizations with concepts that will help them review their existing planning and implementation process. This publication, as well as CWLA's revised *Cultural Competence Self-Assessment Instrument*, assist agencies as they move to integrate cultural competence principles and improve practices.

Reference

U.S. Bureau of the Census. (2001). *Population profile of the United States: 1999* (Current Population Reports, Series P23–205). Washington, DC: U.S. Government Printing Office.

Why Is Cultural Competence Relevant to an Agency?

CHAPTER 1

In 1995, CWLA developed an initiative to help member agencies move toward *cultural competence*—the ability of individuals and systems to respond respectfully and effectively to people of all cultures, races, ethnicities, sexual orientations, and faiths or religions in a manner that recognizes, affirms, and values their worth and protects their dignity. CWLA endeavored to design a flexible, adaptable framework to assist agencies in developing and implementing strategies to integrate cultural competence into the overall organizational strategic planning process.

As part of this initiative, CWLA set out to develop products that would assist human service organizations in integrating cultural competence into their child welfare programs, policies, and cultures. CWLA began the process as we recommend that you begin yours. First, we had a vision. That vision is the belief that to effectively and efficiently serve the increasingly diverse population of this country, child welfare organizations need to become more culturally aware, responsive, and competent.

CWLA's mission was to hold facilitated discussions, communication sessions, and workshops; develop written guides; and conduct consultations that would assist CWLA in advancing cultural competence efforts. To establish cultural competency foundations, CWLA set forth the following goals:

- Promote the understanding of cultural competence as an integral part of best practice in child welfare.
- Develop a process that would assist child welfare agencies in moving toward cultural competence.
- Enable child welfare administrators and managers to lead in including cultural issues as they plan for organizational change.
- Begin ongoing efforts that make effective consultation in cultural competence for child welfare agencies more accessible.

At this point, we must acknowledge the essential tools that enabled us to fulfill our mission and see our vision become reality, and the standards by which decisions in the process were made: our values. The values CWLA used in developing the *Advancing Cultural Competence in Child Welfare* initiative are:

- Cultural competence is for everyone.
- Cultural competence is integral to best practice.
- Cultural competence is ongoing.
- Cultural competence is part of the overall organizational goal of excellence.
- Culturally competent organizations must be customer-driven.
- Cultural competence is a key factor to continued financial survival.
- Culturally competent organizations foster leadership throughout the organization.

Once CWLA developed its mission, goals, and core values, the next challenge was to build the case for change. Child welfare agencies needed a compelling reason to include cultural competence in their strategic planning process.

Cultural competence is important for many reasons. Some are reflected in the history of child welfare in the United States, and in the current status of the racial and ethnic composition of this country.

Over the past 35 years, the United States has experienced a dramatic increase in the number of immigrants and refugees from Latin

America, the Caribbean, Africa, and Asia. All of these people can legitimately call themselves "people of color." Based on a matrix of respondents' answers, Census 2000 researchers created the following race categories: white, black or African American, American Indian or Alaska Native, Asian, Native Hawaiian and other Pacific Islander, and other (Cole, 2002).

In the 2000 Census, African Americans remained the largest group of color. Currently, Hispanics/Latinos are the second largest group (Rosenblatt, 2001a). Experts predict that Hispanics/Latinos will be largest group of people of color in this country by the year 2010 (Morganthau, 1995). This was confirmed by projections made by Rosenblatt (2001a), who analyzed the 2000 Census data.

The Asian population experienced the largest growth, from 2.8% in 1990 to 4.5% in 2000 (Rosenblatt, 2001c). The American Indian population nearly doubled; however, most of its growth is attributed to new criteria that allows people of mixed heritage to select more than one racial group (Rosenblatt, 2001c). More than 2% of the population used this option, which accounts for the vastly different results and interpretation of results in the 2000 Census (Schmitt, 2002).

The U.S. population increased 13.2% overall since the 1990 Census. This is the largest census-to-census increase in American history (U.S. Bureau of the Census, 2001). Although all geographic regions of the country grew, the most significant growth was a 19% increase in the western United States (Rosenblatt, 2001b).

Clearly, the United States is more diverse today than at any other time in history. As this country continues to acknowledge the mixed heritages of many people who live here, it is imperative that child welfare and other human service professionals understand cultural differences and become proficient at integrating the positive aspects of culture into policy, procedures, and service delivery.

Unlike many of their predecessors, some immigrant and refugee groups entering the United States today do not seek assimilation and acculturation into the American mainstream. They do not want to become "Americans" at the cost of losing their own heritage. They learn how to balance both cultures and function in both worlds.

The infusion of these immigrant and refugee cultures into the American mainstream has resulted in many native-born Americans' redefining their cultural descriptors in terms of their ancestral heritage, instead of generic designation, such as black or white. Americans have become more concerned about the cultures of their ancestry. They value the richness of diversity that comprises their personal cultures.

Just as diversity has changed the look of the nation, it has dramatically changed the look of the workforce in the United States (Gerber, 1990). To remain competitive in the marketplace, both for-profit and nonprofit organizations have had to reevaluate how they operate.

Cultural competence in the workplace is more important to for-profit and nonprofit organizations in the new millennium. Changes in the demographic composition of the workforce require corresponding changes in organizational culture. To reap the rewards of having culturally competent staff, organizations need to be flexible and look for new ways to include diverse communities in organizational planning.

To prepare for the integration of cultural competence principles into their organization's strategic plan, child welfare agencies should

- assess the costs and benefits of integrating cultural competence into the vision, mission, values, goals, policies, procedures, program designs, and outcomes of the agency; and
- reach consensus as to why an integrated comprehensive approach is the best way to ensure that cultural competence becomes part of the organizational culture.

The systemic, long-term valuing of cultural competence requires agency-wide commitment to an ongoing review of organizational culture. This professional and organizational commitment begins with the agency leaders. They must commit resources—time, people, and money—and make personal and professional commitments to advance cultural competence in the organization. In addition, leaders must take responsibility for working with the board of directors or governing body to start the change process. With this approach, employees may better understand the ongoing nature of the process and the need for each person to have a role in moving the organization toward overall competence—a component of which is cultural competence.

References

Cole, Y. (2002, January 18). *New census demographics: Multiracial Americans increase, most live on West Coast.* Available from http://www.diversityinc.com/members/1835.cfm.

Gerber, B. (1990, July 24). Managing diversity. *Training*, p. 24.

Morganthau, T. (1995, February 13). What color is black? *Newsweek*, p. 64.

Rosenblatt, R. (2001a, March 7). Administration says 2000 Census a "quality count," won't be adjusted. *Los Angeles Times*, A6.

Rosenblatt, R. (2001b, April 3). America's bumper crop: All 50 states show populations gains. *Los Angeles Times*, A5.

Rosenblatt, R. (2001c, March 13). Census illustrated diversity from sea to shinning sea. *Los Angeles Times*, A16.

Schmitt, E. (2002, February 12). For 7 million people in Census one race category isn't enough. *Crossing Cultures—The Multi-Racial American.* Available from http://www.silkrc.com/Xcultures/census.htm.

U.S. Bureau of the Census, U.S. Department of Commerce. (2001, April). *U.S. Census 2000 population change and distribution Census 2000 brief.* Washington, DC: Author.

How Have Agencies Served People of Color in the Past?

CHAPTER 2

The field of social work in general, and the child welfare system in particular, have a history of exclusion and disparity in service delivery for children and families of color. This chapter discusses the struggles African Americans, Native Americans, and Latinos have experienced in the child welfare system.

African Americans

In the 1960s, the civil rights movement spawned a climate for the development of voluntary agencies to serve African American children and families. Participation by African Americans on the boards of these agencies gave African Americans their first opportunity to control the services delivered to their children and families (Hogan & Siu, 1988).

Billingsley and Giovannoni (as cited in Hogan & Siu, 1988) hypothesized that three factors caused the increased inclusion of African Americans in the child welfare system after World War II:

> (1) The increased migration by black families to the North, (2) the public system increasingly caring for more poor minority children as the number of poor white children decreased, and (3) the effects of a new national focus on integration. (p. 494)

Billingsley and Giovannoni (as cited in Hogan & Siu, 1988) believed, however, that the child welfare system continued to treat children of color differently. They believed that "racism was manifested in three ways—by the kinds of services developed, by inequitable treatment based on race within the service delivery system, and by incomplete efforts to change the system" (p. 494). They concluded that although workers made a concerted effort to eliminate discriminatory practices in child welfare in the 1970s, an unfair distribution of services remained. This continued to prevent African American children and families from receiving adequate services.

Billingsley and Giovannoni (as cited in Hogan & Siu, 1988) proposed that child welfare develop a pluralistic, multiethnic service delivery system to address the needs of all children. Although workers increased and improved access to services for children of color, disparity in resource allocation is still a problem. Stenho's review of Shyne and Shroeder's data collected in 1978 indicated that "greater proportions of African American children were served in the public sector...and that Caucasian parents received more social service support than other parents" (as cited in Courtney et al., 1996, p. 108).

Native Americans

The child welfare system has been particularly devastating to Native American children and families. In 1977, 1% of the children in the child welfare system were Native Americans. The Children's Defense Fund (as cited in Hogan & Siu, 1988) reported that this constituted overrepresentation based on the number of Native American children in the total population. Unger's research (as cited in Hogan & Siu, 1988) showed that surveys conducted between 1969 and 1974 "documented that between 25% and 35% of all Native American children were placed in foster or adoptive homes or institutions" (p. 494). Byler's (1977) research indicated that 80% of those placements were in Caucasian homes.

Unger (as cited in Hogan & Siu, 1988) noted that teachers did not allow Native American children in the boarding school system to use their native languages or observe cultural customs. Also, a high percentage of transracial placements occurred because Native American families faced insurmountable obstacles in meeting the dominant culture's qualifications to be foster and adoptive parents. Olsen's (1982) analysis of Shyne and Shroeder's data indicated that Native American children were the least likely to be recommended for services, whereas Caucasian and Asian children were most likely to receive services. Although controversial and problematic, the passage of the Indian Child Welfare Act in 1978 at least stemmed the tide of Native American children being placed in homes where they are estranged from their culture.

Latinos

> Latinos in the U.S. come from primarily 20 different countries in Latin America. Although they may share a common language and selected aspects of the Spanish and Latin America cultures, they are not a homogenous group. All Latinos have a different set of behaviors, customs and values depending [on] their cultural heritage, upbringing, life experiences or the circumstances under which they came to the United States. (Illinois Department of Children and Family Services, 1996, p. 2)

Language and other cultural issues have created barriers for Latino children and families in accessing services. Traditionally, Latino children have been transracially placed: Workers placed lighter skinned children with Caucasian families and darker skinned children with African American families (Montalvo, 1994).

This devaluation of their cultures has negatively affected Latino children and may be the reason for so many being labeled "behaviorally disturbed." Latino people have a wide variety of cultures, which makes placing Latino children more challenging. Placing Latino children in culturally inappropriate homes can further estrange them from their cultures and may cause difficulties in their acculturating with their foster or adoptive families.

Latino children younger than 7 were less likely to have service plans than any other group of children (Montalvo, 1994). African American and Latino children were least likely to have contact with family members, although their family members were often interested in visiting the children. Workers were more likely to assess Latino adolescents as having behavioral problems, and Latino teens were most likely to be placed in group homes (Montalvo, 1994, p. 8).

References

Byler, W. (1977). The destruction of American Indian families. In S. Unger (Ed.), *The destruction of American Indian families* (pp. 1–11). New York: Association on American Indian Affairs.

Courtney, M. E., Barth, R. P., Berrick, J. D., Brooks, D., Needell, R., & Park, L. (1996). Race and child welfare services: Past research and future directions. *Child Welfare, 75,* 99–137.

Hogan, P. T., & Siu, S.-F. (1988, November/December). Minority children and the child welfare system: An historical perspective. *Social Work, 33,* 493–498.

Illinois Department of Children and Family Services. (1996, December). *Hispanic family profile.* Chicago: Author.

Montalvo, E. (1994). Against all odds: The challenges faced by Latino families and children in the United States. *Roundtable,* p. 8.

Olsen, L. J. (1982). Predicting the permanency status of children in foster care. *Social Work Research & Abstracts, 18,* 9–20.

Challenges and Benefits of Cultural Competence

When deciding to include cultural competence in their strategic plans, organizations must weigh the difficulties against the benefits.

Difficulties Integrating Cultural Competence

Each organization's issues may be different. Some common difficulties with cultural competence are:

- Cultural competence is hard work.
- No blueprint exists for cultural competence.
- Cultural competence requires ongoing commitments of money, time, and people.
- Cultural competence is a constant effort—room always exists for improvement.
- Cultural competence goals may require revisions to programs, policies, and procedures, or shifts in organizational culture.
- Cultural competence is costly, because staff members need to go through awareness and skills-based education.
- Organizational size and hierarchical structure can complicate the integration of cultural competence principles.

Benefits of Cultural Competence

Whatever difficulties agencies may face in working to integrate cultural competence principles, they will receive long-term benefits.

Culturally competent agencies
- are customer-driven, and therefore, understand and respond to the needs of the populations they serve;
- reflect the population served in their staffing and their physical environment;
- value their employees and seek to make them more active in decisions that affect external customers;
- design programs, policies, and procedures that are sensitive and effective in meeting the needs of the population served in a manner that is most beneficial and acceptable to that population;
- balance the needs of the organization, employees, and population served to achieve optimal results;
- attract a larger applicant pool to fill vacancies, because the organization is perceived as a safe place for those seeking a supportive work environment;
- are more desirable candidates for funders, who are increasingly including cultural competence as a component in grant guidelines; and
- are more likely to receive referrals from other organizations that need to secure assistance and support for the increasingly diverse populations presenting for services.

Why Include Cultural Competence in a Strategic Plan?

CHAPTER 4

Organizations should view cultural competence as an integral part of their strategic planning process. Introducing cultural competence principles to an organization as a single initiative could give the impression that cultural competence is a special program that will have a definite timeline for completion.

The integration of cultural competence objectives should be deliberate, cross-functional, and long term. Although employees' agreement to change is necessary, it is not sufficient to initiate or sustain the process. Ongoing commitment from management *is* essential. Each level of the organization has to be engaged in the process, beginning with the board of directors or governing body.

A systematic and comprehensive approach is the most effective way of integrating cultural competence into every facet of the organization. A fragmented approach fails to build a strong foundation for cultural competence. Administration of programs, organizational priorities, and the basis on which decisions are made affect the cultural competence of an organization. Programs should be administered relative to the needs of the population receiving the services. Organizational priorities and expected outcomes govern how the organization allocates resources. If cultural competence is not a strategic priority, it will not be integrated into the operations of the agency. Moving toward cultural competence requires deliberate planning and should translate into changes in individual and organizational behaviors with demonstrable results.

It is also important for organizations to understand that like any ongoing process, cultural competence goals require periodic review and assessment. Using an assessment tool to perform periodic reviews ensures that goals are comprehensive and will assist in documenting progress and charting a future course (see Chapter 5 for information on assessment).

To meet the needs of increasingly diverse populations effectively and efficiently, child welfare agencies must use a multipronged approach. A diverse and culturally competent staff is important, however, without a strategic planning process that integrates cultural competence principles and goals, the agency's goals will be difficult to attain. Building on a supportive strategic plan, the agency should develop policies that support programmatic goals that are flexible enough to incorprate the nuances of cultural diversity.

Stretegic plans must be appropriate and applicable for the populations served to ensure that each individual, family, and community receives services and supports that help them achieve their full potential. From the time a child or family enters the agency, they should encounter people who have the skills to address their needs in a culturally competent and appropriate manner. They need to feel understood, respected, and safe.

How Does an Agency Evaluate Itself?

CHAPTER 5

The first step in a strategic planning process is to assess what the agency wants to accomplish. For cultural competence, asking the following questions may help:

- Is the goal to value diversity or to manage diversity?
- Is the goal to learn more about diversity?
- Is the goal to become more efficient and effective in providing services?
- Is the goal to create an environment that fosters open discussion about differences and in which differences are openly addressed in the decisionmaking process for children and families?
- How can the agency assess and measure the cultural competence of policies, programs, and service delivery plans currently in use?
- What types of ongoing staff education and development are needed to improve understanding of the importance of cultural competence at the agency, for the populations served, and in the work staff do every day?
- Are regulatory authorities' and funders' guidelines or criteria placing expectations on issues of cultural competence as part of their requirements?
- Is the agency aware of the needs of the populations served? How does the agency know this?

Having a formal assessment process will help evaluate the entire organization. In addition, conducting an assessment will help prioritize steps in the process. Using a cultural competence assessment tool, such as CWLA's revised *Cultural Competence Self-Assessment Instrument*, will not only help determine the organization's readiness for change, but will also guide long-term planning.

An effective cultural competence assessment tool should evaluate the following:

- **The vision, mission, and core values of the organization.** These values guide the organization and are the foundation on which managers make decisions about service goals and the organization's general direction. The values should be consistent in promoting culturally competent and appropriate programs, policies, and practice.

- **The composition of the governing body or board of directors.** The governing body leads the organization and establishes its priorities. Commitment to and support for the cultural competence process are essential for success. The governing body must be dedicated to cultural competence and consistently seek to reflect the diversity of the organization and population served in its membership. This will send a strong message that cultural competence is important to the organization. A governing body that values cultural competence will also be more effective in developing a strategic plan to effectively meet the needs of diverse communities. To the extent possible, governing bodies should recruit members from the communities served, as well as representatives from other stakeholder groups.

- **The selection process for governing body members.** The criteria that are used to select governing body members can affect its diversity. Who is solicited for membership? What is done to connect new members to the group and retain established members can determine whether it achieves cultural competence goals.

- **Governing body orientation and ongoing education.** In this constantly changing environment, ongoing education is important to keep abreast of what is occurring in communities and how the organization can align itself to meet the changing needs of the population served.
- **Criteria on which leaders are selected to run the organization.** Because the role of the executive is complex, most organizations believe that there is a small pool of qualified candidates. Qualified people with good ideas and the ability to make them happen, however, live in a variety of communities. To reach this pool of talent, organizations need to be creative in their search process. Sometimes organizations establish requirements for leadership positions that screen out interested and capable candidates. Length of time in a leadership position does not necessarily equal success in the position.

Leadership

Looking for the following skills is useful in selecting a leader who values cultural competence:

- the ability to create a climate for excellence;
- the ability to provide a safe environment for discussion of culture and constructive exchange of diverse ideas and information;
- the ability to inspire and motivate people;
- the ability to take risks with comfort;
- a belief that customer service and satisfaction, both internal and external, are the most important factors in a healthy organization; and
- a belief that change is inevitable and should be embraced and encouraged.

These are desirable qualities for any person being hired in a managerial capacity. A person who values cultural competence, however, will use these strengths to enhance the organization by bringing training and new voices to the organization. This person will be the catalyst for diversifying staff; creating innovative programs, policy, and practice; improving communication throughout the organization; and encouraging more interaction with the population served in ways that improve outcomes.

Leaders must be personally dedicated to the constant growth and development of cultural competence skills and knowledge. The need to get people to deliver the desired results is essential. A leader's personality and values are key factors in determining whether he or she can achieve the organization's desired results. Someone who can integrate cultural competence principles into the organization's vision, mission, and values will be in a better position to meet the organization' s expectations.

Programs, Policies, and Practices

To successfully deliver culturally competent services and supports, agencies must ensure internal policies and procedures are culturally competent. It is not enough to send line staff and supervisors to cultural competence or diversity education sessions. The organization needs to have an agency-wide goal of cultural competence, including making appropriate educational sessions available to all internal stakeholders, improving relationships with the community, developing effective policies, and designing programs and case management systems that are appropriate and applicable to the population served.

Policies, Procedures, and Personnel

Policies and procedures should be flexible. Part of valuing culture is understanding that flexibility is important. Organizations and service providers need to be creative and willing to engage service populations in creating policies and procedures. In addition, personnel manuals are important to cultivating and maintaining cultural competence in the workplace. Cultural competence should be a consideration throughout an employee's tenure with an organization. Cultural competence principles should also be included in job descriptions and should be a central consideration in performance evaluations, disciplinary actions, work hours, and leave policies.

Program Development

Flexibility should be a key ingredient in development of programs. Programs that are responsive to the needs of the population served have better outcomes for the customer and the staff. Information gathered in customer satisfaction surveys or focus groups can be helpful in this process. Including all levels of staff and consumer representation on program design committees will also help ensure that the agency meets the needs and expectations of both internal and external customers.

Case Management

Services are to be delivered with respect, ultimately seeking to build on family strengths. Workers should develop service plans in partnership with families, acknowledging that families know their needs. Agencies should establish clear responsibilities with regard to both family and agency activities. Attention to accessibility of appropriate services should be consistent.

Recruitment and Retention

Organizations should be innovative in how they recruit for vacancies. To enhance diversity, organizations should consider using media and publications that target specific groups and relationships with community organizations to enhance their ability to hire staff who are culturally diverse and competent. To retain employees, organizations must create an environment in which culture is valued and discussion of diversity is safe and constructive.

In addition, some incentives that organizations can offer attract and maintain staff. For example, mentoring and career pathing are two options. Mentoring programs are helpful in assisting new employees to adjust to the organization. Mentoring is a vehicle through which the organization can communicate the organizational vision, mission, and goals.

Career paths can be used by organizations to retain employees. Career paths require a considerable amount of planning, but can have long-term results. To be effective, each position in the organization should have a career path—an established advancement and development path for staff to move vertically in the organization. This can be shared with new employees as a benefit of joining the organization.

Community and Public Image

Agencies can create an atmosphere of familiarity and safety by having staff who are reflective of the population served. In addition, agencies can use furnishings and artwork to reflect the cultural values of the children and families who present for services. Even the magazines ordered for reception areas can contribute to the creation of a safe and hospitable environment.

Agencies that are able to create a safe and comfortable environment are more likely to attract a diverse client population and are more likely to receive referrals from other human service agencies. In this way, cultural competence affects the fiscal health of the agency.

The perception of the organization in the community and the location of the agency can be factors in determining who applies for positions and who requests services. Organizations that cultivate relationships with the communities they serve (i.e., that participate on community advisory boards, establish relationships with faith communities or civic groups, and serve on agency boards and committees) are more culturally competent and linguistically appropriate when meeting the needs of staff and communities.

Publications

Publications should reflect the populations served in content and design. Publications in different languages, with photographs, graphics, or other artwork, should reflect the diversity of the population served. In addition, publications should be designed to have the most positive effect on those who will read them.

Outcome Evaluations

As child welfare agencies become more outcomes based, they need to establish evaluation guidelines. It is important for child welfare agencies and professionals to know how the populations they serve are affected by the programs administered. Agencies should identify desired outcomes for each program area. These outcomes should be measurable and relate to how children and families are affected. The delivery of appropriate services that produce desired outcomes is cost effective. Delivering services that do not meet the needs of the population ultimately means that additional services will be required to produce the desired results.

Advocacy

Often, the child welfare agency has an interest in both providing services to children and families and in advocating in their behalf. Service workers may advocate for customers in seeking needed services from other agencies (i.e., health care, special education, parenting support). Service organizations can advocate in behalf of a population of families in the public policy area. Child welfare executives and managers may find that a specific cultural issue is the driving force behind the decision to initiate advocacy. Potentially, many will benefit from this effort spurred by a few, when the result is more respectful, effective, and relevant services for children and families.

Internal and External Customer Feedback

Organizations that are effective in any change process have solicited, received, and made revisions based on the feedback of internal and external customers. Organizations that have long-term growth credit keeping an open ear to their customers as the reason they continue to be successful in the marketplace. External customers are the ultimate judge of effectiveness, however, internal customers have valuable insight into how to improve services, because they have a dual vantage point. Front-line staff who deliver services are aware of organizational goals and intentions, as well as the perceptions and effectiveness of agency services. This information can help agencies focus the change process. It also makes both internal and external customers feel valued and important to the organization and feel they are included in the ongoing process.

Volunteer Recruitment, Selection, and Orientation

Volunteers have an important and unique role in child welfare organizations. Although their desire to provide assistance is an asset to the agency, the volunteers' lack of formal connection to the agency may present some challenges. It is important that volunteers understand and are a suitable fit with the agency's mission, values, goals, objectives, and culture. Volunteers should be included in the plan to integrate cultural competence into the strategic plan.

Volunteers should possess the same interpersonal skills required of staff members, especially if they will have contact with the children and families served by the agency. The agency should establish evaluative criteria to ensure that volunteers are a good fit with the organization and the tasks they will perform. In addition, the agency should include volunteers in in-service training and ongoing developmental training, evaluation, and feedback processes.

Recruitment, Orientation, and Training of Foster and Adoptive Parents

Foster and adoptive parents hold key roles in the child welfare system. Children unable to remain in their own home must have a safe, stable, nurturing home with another family. As caregivers, foster and adoptive parents will play a critical role in the development of the child; therefore, the selection, orientation, and training of these caregivers will directly affect the health, welfare, and happiness of the children. Although debate continues about transracial placements and adoptions, it is clear that children thrive in stable, caring, loving homes.

CWLA emphasizes the early achievement of an appropriate permanency goal for each child. CWLA further encourages agencies to make every effort to place children in homes that are consistent with the child's ethnicity and culture, past identifications, and living experiences. When all reasonable efforts have been made over a period of time to find parents of the same ethnicity and culture as the child, CWLA supports the identification of another suitable family to provide a home for the child. When a child is placed transracially, however, agencies should assess the ability of the foster and adoptive parents to access cultural resources to support the child and family after the placement.

The ability of an agency to recruit and retain a diverse pool of foster and adoptive parents who can create and maintain an environment that is supportive to the total development of a child is invaluable. Recruiting guidelines for foster and adoptive parents should reflect the understanding that several factors make a good parent, a good home, and a good family. There is no "model family" that creates the best environment for the rearing of children. Single parents, gay and lesbian parents, parents who work outside the home, and parents who do not earn a lot of money should not be excluded from consideration.

All foster and adoptive parents should be trained to deal with the many feelings and issues that arise by opening their home to a foster or adoptive child. Agencies should require that they demonstrate flexibility and resourcefulness in assisting the child to connect with his or her culture. Even where no racial or ethnic difference exists between adoptive or foster parent and child, other cultural issues may require the foster or adoptive parent to be resourceful in creating a healthy, loving, and stable environment for the child.

Organizational Culture

Every organization has norms, values, and beliefs that make up its culture. How the organization functions is part of its culture. Agencies striving for cultural competence want to attain a level of openness that supports discussion of difference. The organizational culture has to value difference, learning, and change. Successful agencies replace the "that's the way we have always done it" mentality with an "if it makes us more efficient, effective, and responsive, let's work on it" mentality.

Needs of the Population

When assessing the needs of the population it serves, an organization must consider several factors. Individual culture is shaped by a variety of factors. An individual's racial and ethnic group may not be the aspect of the culture with which he or she most strongly identifies. Therefore, when an organization designs policies, procedures, personnel manuals, programs, service delivery plans, publications, and so forth, it should consider the following aspects of culture:

- religion and spiritual beliefs
- language
- age
- education
- gender roles
- intergenerational dynamics
- beliefs about receiving help from outside the family
- parenting norms
- beliefs about health care
- sexual orientation
- mental health issues
- physical challenges and vision or hearing impairment
- racism
- ethnicity

- geographic location of the organization
- time period when individuals were born
- geographic location of rearing and/or current location of home
- family values
- self-determination
- placement in sibling group
- race

The assessment process can be extremely complex, but it is the foundation for learning and understanding who works in and who is served by the organization. The time it takes to collect these data will be well worth the effort to get an accurate picture of the agency as it goes through the process of achieving cultural competence.

How Does an Agency Develop an Action Plan?

CHAPTER 6

O nce the organization has completed an initial assessment, it must develop an action plan. The decisions made in developing the plan and the priority assigned to each task will grow out of the recommendations and information gathered in the assessment process.

The action plan should consist of realistic tasks and timelines. Most important, the action plan should be inclusive, assigning tasks to staff at all levels of the organization. Inclusion through communication and involvement will increase employees' ownership of the process and build loyalty to the organization while promoting unity both horizontally and vertically. All stakeholder groups should be represented in the process and be active participants in transforming the organization.

Distribute leadership, accountability, and responsibility among the entire staff. Allowing those not normally in leadership roles to be responsible for the development, design, and implementation of parts of the process will encourage staff to be concerned about the agency as a whole, as opposed to just the area in which they work.

Leaders in the organization should give line staff opportunities to be decisionmakers. Empower employees to use their creativity and insight to design more culturally competent policies, programs, and practice directives. Organizations get strength from including the thoughts, concerns, and insights of staff who are generally not decisionmakers. Do not overlook resources and assets, and do not miss an opportunity to foster leadership throughout the organization!

The action plan should address dilemmas facing the organization that have cultural implications, which should have surfaced during the assessment process. A manager can get additional information from customer satisfaction surveys and discussions of focus groups developed for each stakeholder group.

Any change is gradual and takes time. All stakeholders must be part of the process from planning to implementation, and it is crucial that tasks and timelines be realistic. If the manager gets sidetracked, a good plan will help bring the process back in line. Change can sometimes be painful and difficult in organizations. Keep in mind, however, that without change there cannot be growth.

How Does Change Happen?

CHAPTER 7

Child welfare and human service professionals must continually embrace cultural change. Their job is to make sure that the future of children is better in the next decade than it is now. The future of America includes an increasingly diverse population. Taking steps to meet the new challenges now will prepare organizations to continue to champion the cause for children.

For the agency whose goal is to value cultural diversity, two change processes must occur simultaneously: organizational and behavioral.

Organizational Change

The change process that helps organizations integrate cultural competence is much the same as any change management strategy. Although the steps may be the same, the outcome should be driven by a desire to build an organization that is not only capable of delivering linguistically and culturally appropriate services, but also has policies and practices that create a safe and supportive environment for diverse internal stakeholders. Cultural competence principles should be integrated throughout the agency at every level, in every program, and in all practices.

Development of culturally competent programs and policies needs to be inclusive and take into account the perspectives of all stakeholders. Some primary steps are:

- Evaluate current conditions and decide what needs to be changed.
- Develop a case or compelling reason to support why change needs to occur.
- Develop a plan to achieve the change.
- Generate discussion within the organization about the reasons for change. Such discussion will facilitate the commitment of everyone in the organization.
- Create results-oriented, long-term strategies for achieving change.
- Institute mechanisms to keep change process moving and on target, as well as to collect and respond to feedback.
- Involve key stakeholders in the process and give them specific tasks to ensure commitment and success.
- Make sure that resources (money, time, people, policies, and procedures) are in place to assist the organization in facilitating change and attaining desired results.
- Integrate the changes into the operations of the organization.
- Evaluate at regular intervals for modification and reinforcement.
- Continuously look for ways to improve the organizational culture, operations, and practices.

Behavioral Change

Organizations are built by and for people. The integration of cultural competence principles by agencies requires shifts in organizational and individual behavior. The normal process of this change includes:

- A change in thinking and acceptance of different attitudes, beliefs, values, and perceptions;
- A change in actions, accompanied by a clear and realistic plan for changing practice; and
- A change in habit as the commitment to the new way of thinking and acting increases.

Relationships between stakeholders will evolve, individually and collectively, to achieve sustained movement toward cultural competence. This can be assisted by

- introducing a catalyst for change;
- processing the new information and evaluate how it challenges established thoughts, beliefs, values, and behaviors;
- deciding what kind of action should be taken to modify or correct behavior to be in line with the new environment; and
- practicing the new actions and thinking patterns until they become a habit that is then integrated into behaviors.

Other Factors in the Change Process

In addition, organizations have other factors to consider. These will have affect how decisions are made, what services are provided, and how best outcomes can be attained.

Race and ethnicity are the two most obvious concerns in cultural competence, because they are the easiest to recognize. Many of the issues that surround cultural competence clearly result from differences in race and ethnicity. Majority and minority orientation conflicts are the root of many problems experienced between people. There are no easy answers to this problem, and it continues to be an emotional and provocative issue. Organizations and individuals should recognize that there are many other factors that can play a role, and they should investigate the possibility that these factors can complicate the ability to provide services.

Intergenerational and Gender Roles

A hierarchical family structure governs interactions between family members and with those outside the family. It is important for child welfare organizations and professionals to understand that these dynamics exist and learn to work within the family structure. Child welfare professionals should ascertain who is the head or leader of the family unit and work with them to give assistance to the child and the remainder of the family.

Having positive and effective interactions with children and families requires that child welfare organizations and professionals respect family structures and design policies, procedures, and case management plans that are easily adaptable to a wide range of family structures and dynamics. The person who needs to obtain services may not be the person first contacted. Ignoring those who are not readily apparent as important in the family structure may create distrust and may cause families to be noncompliant with the management plan.

Education

A person's education level usually determines his or her ability to survive economically. Formal education, however, does not ensure the ability to provide appropriate parenting, and, conversely, lack of education does not equate to poor parenting skills. In addition, a parent's affluence has no direct correlation to their parenting quality. Child welfare organizations and professionals, therefore, should look for other criteria that can assist them in making decisions about parents' abilities to provide adequate parenting.

Parenting

Parenting roles vary widely between cultures—what may be acceptable in one may be perceived as inappropriate or harmful in another. When confronted with different methods of parenting, child welfare professionals should seek to understand the purpose of the parent's behavior in response to the child's. Once a child welfare professional understands the purpose for the parent's behavior, a more informed case management plan can be drafted and more appropriate services given to the child and family.

Language and Communication

When language barriers exist, it is not a good idea to have a child serve as an interpreter, because this places the child in an adult role and involves him or her in an adult conversation. In addition, it is difficult and traumatic for a child if he or she must translate for his or her abuser. This makes the parent feel powerless and resentful of the process. For these cases, a bilingual staff member or interpreter will make interaction with the family go more smoothly. Organizations should become familiar with federal policies regarding limited English proficiency service provision (see Title VI of the Civil Rights Act of 1964).

Whether the barrier is a different language or a visual or hearing impairment, organizations need to make provisions for communicating with children and families through the medium that is most comfortable for them. This can be accomplished by providing training and encouraging staff to be bilingual, and by hiring bilingual staff and those skilled in sign language. If staff cannot fulfill these needs, then the agencies should contract for translation.

In addition, publications about the agency and the services offered should be developed in the language of the population served (i.e., in Braille, on audiotape, in Spanish, etc.).

Communication styles and patterns differ by cultural group. Child welfare professionals should be aware that these differences exist and identify the best way to communicate with the populations served by the agency.

Homelessness

Homelessness is a growing problem in this country, with families being the fastest growing segment of the homeless population. Providing a safe, stable, loving, and nurturing environment is difficult enough. Homelessness creates a set of complex challenges that require agencies and child welfare professionals to be more innovative and flexible in their approach to achieving positive outcomes.

Sexual Orientation

Sexual orientation has been at the root of many custody battles. Research indicates, however, that gay and lesbian birthparents, adoptive parents, and foster parents are just as capable of providing a caring, nurturing, and stable home as heterosexual parents. Agencies need to consider gays and lesbians as viable and appropriate choices for providing homes for children.

Research has shown that gay, lesbian, bisexual, transgender, and questioning youth are more likely to be depressed and attempt or commit suicide. They sustain more abuse from peers and are often ostracized by their families. Child welfare professionals should provide support and link these youth to sources of support in the community.

Religion

Religion, spirituality, and faith play major roles in some cultures in determining how children are reared, how family members interact with one another, and how they interact with people outside the family. It is important for human service professionals to respect this and take into account the religious, spiritual, and faith-based practices of families when designing programs, policies, and procedures.

Health Care

Beliefs about health care can create barriers in providing services to families. These beliefs often stem from cultural or traditional beliefs, lack of education, fear of strangers and large systems, or language barriers. Organizations and child welfare professionals should first identify the reason the family is not seeking health care and then work with the family and health care providers to achieve the best outcome, while respecting the cultural and religious beliefs of the family.

Juvenile Justice

Juvenile justice documents that youth of color who commit or are accused of delinquent acts are more likely to be adjudicated in the juvenile justice system, whereas children of white European descent are usually given mental health services. Because of the disproportionate effect this trend has on communities of color, child welfare professionals need to work in conjunction with the juvenile justice and education systems to evaluate the criteria with which workers make decisions. Failure to find more appropriate solutions or alternatives to juvenile detention will allow the increase in the number of children of color being reared in correctional facilities to continue.

How Does an Agency Involve the Community?

CHAPTER 8

Image is everything! How the community views an agency will affect the agency's ability to positively affect outcomes for children and families.

If the population served perceives that the agency does not understand their needs or concerns, case management planning will be difficult. Organizations must value and respect communities to be valued and respected themselves. Being involved in the community also allows the community to be involved in the organization. Recognizing the community as an important stakeholder in the change process and inviting members to participate in the development of cultural competence principles is an excellent step toward building a relationship with the community. This also gives the agency valuable information about community needs and expectations. Some strategies that can enhance community relationships are:

- Invite community members to the agency to learn about the staff, services, and operations.
- Survey the families served and the local community for feedback about services, needs, and expectations.
- Ask community leaders to sit on the board of directors or other agency task forces and committees.
- Conduct periodic focus groups and other activities to get input from the community about agency practice and suggestions for improvement.

- Participate in community functions and cultural activities and, when possible, work collaboratively or in partnership with community groups.
- Volunteer as members of community advisory boards and civic groups.
- Invite community members to periodically brief the board of directors about services, needs, and expectations.
- Establish formal liaisons between the organization and the community.
- Focus recruitment efforts to increase the number of staff from the community.
- Provide opportunities to include volunteers from the community.

How Does an Agency Practice Cultural Competence Among Its Staff?

CHAPTER 9

Providing services for children, youth, and families that meet their needs is the ultimate goal for any child welfare agency. To meet that goal, the organization has to begin with itself and develop good internal customer service.

What is internal customer service? Organizations have internal customers, either as individuals or as departments. Each individual or group has customers and is also a customer to other individuals or divisions or departments. The interdependency of the organization creates the customer relationships. Each person needs information, services, or products from another to perform effectively and achieve desired outcomes.

Some examples of internal customer relationships are the person who orders the supplies and the individual who requests supplies; or the worker who receives a case and the worker who transfers the case. Another example is the executive who sees the need for a change in organizational operations and organizes a multidisciplinary group to decide what the change affects, how the change will be accomplished, what the expected outcomes are, and what role each person in the organization will play.

Some of the same factors that are important in understanding and valuing culture in the development of programs, policies, and procedures are equally important in the recruitment and retention of staff. As the workforce becomes more culturally diverse, a new set of factors will affect what motivates employees and how the organization functions.

Race, ethnicity, intergenerational and gender roles, parenting norms, communication, sexual orientation, level of education, and religion will affect the work environment in the same ways they affect decisions made regarding development of programs, policies, and procedures for clients.

Value and respect staff; celebrate and incorporate their cultural strengths and beliefs into how the organization functions. Give consideration to these values when personnel policies and procedures are being drafted, when job descriptions are written, when the holiday schedule is determined, and so forth.

Success in the cultural competence change process means that everyone in an organization is willing to learn about other cultures and allow for the adjustments that are necessary as the agency moves toward cultural competence goals.

Conclusion

C ultural competence is a process. It requires a long-term commitment of resources—money, people, and time—to be successful. Organizations striving to implement cultural competence principles need to plan, be persistent, and remain flexible. As organizations evolve their cultural competence goals, they will encounter other external forces that challenge their ability to deliver appropriate and relevant services.

Making cultural competence an organizational priority, however, is a part of overall organizational competence. The integration of cultural competence in the strategic planning process is integral to developing best practices and has implications for fiscal survival. Cultural competence is an inclusive concept and is for everyone. We must work individually and collectively to understand, respect, and celebrate the richness that difference brings to our lives and the workplace.

In the new millennium, child welfare agencies must be prepared to meet the increasing demands by both external and internal consumers for appropriate services and supports. As the composition of the general population becomes more diverse, so will the needs of the children and families served by the child welfare system. If child welfare agencies truly want to help each child and family reach its full potential, they must understand culture and diversity. To reach this goal, however, child welfare agencies should know that diversity begins within an organization. Therefore, the agencies that want to attract and retain the best talent in the field must demonstrate the ability to provide a safe and comfortable environment where diverse cultures are valued.

Resources

Disabilities

Beck, R. L. (1989, March). Hearing-impaired social workers: Something lost, something gained. *Social Work, 34,* 151–153.

Luey, H. S., Glass, L., & Elliott, H. (1995, March). Hard-of-hearing or deaf: Issues of ears, language, culture, and identity. *Social Work, 40,* 177–181.

National Council on Disability. (1999, December 1). *Lift every voice: Modernizing disability policies and programs to serve a diverse nation.* Washington, DC: Author.

Sarti, D. M. (1993, March). Reaching the deaf child: A model for diversified intervention. *Smith College Studies in Social Work, 63,* 187–197.

Diversity

Adams, M., Bell, L. A., & Griffin, P. (Eds.). (1997). *Teaching for diversity and social justice: A source book.* New York: Rutledge.

Daly, A. (Ed.). (1998). *Workplace diversity: Issues and perspectives.* Washington, DC: National Association of Social Workers.

Physical and Mental Health

Benjamin, M. (1999). Cultural competence in early identification. *Focal Point, 13*(1), 22–23.

Isaacs, M. R., & Benjamin, M. P. (1991, December). *Towards a culturally competent system of care. Volume II: Programs which utilitize culturally competent principles.* Washington, DC: Natioanl Technical Assistance Center for Children's Mental Health, Center for Child Health and Mental Health Policy, Georgetown University Child Development Center.

Office of National AIDS Policy. (1996, March). *Youth & HIV/AIDS: An American agenda. A report to the President.* Washington, DC: Author.

Spector, R. E. (1996). *Cultural diversity in health and illness* (4th ed.). Stamford, CT: Appleton and Lange.

Stevenson, H. C., Jr. (1994, September). The psychology of sexual racism and AIDS: An ongoing saga of distrust and the sexual other. *Journal of Black Studies, 25,* 62–80.

U.S. Department of Health and Human Services Office of Minority Health. (2001, March). *National standards for culturally and linguistically appropriate services in health care. Final report.* Washington, DC: Author.

Organizational Development

Anthony, D., Carnevale, P., & Stone, S. C. (1994, October). Diversity: Beyond the golden rule. *Training & Development,* 22–39.

Fram, E. F., & Pearse, R. F. (1992). *The high-performance nonprofit: A management guide for boards and executives.* Milwaukee, WI: Family Service America.

Geber, B. (1990, July). Managing diversity. *Training,* 23–30.

Goldstein, J., & Leopold, M. (1990, November). Corporate culture versus ethnic culture. *Personnel Journal,* 83–92.

Jamieson, D., & O'Mara, J. (1991). *Managing Workforce 2000: Gaining the diversity advantage.* San Francisco, CA: Jossey-Bass.

Rutledge, J. M. (1994). *Building board diversity.* Washington, DC: National Center for Nonprofit Boards.

Thomas, D. A., & Ely, R. J. (1996, September/October). Making differences matter: A new paradigm for managing diversity. *Harvard Business Review, 74,* 79–90.

Practice

Ahn, H. N., & Gilbert, N. (1992, September). Cultural diversity and sexual abuse prevention. *Social Service Review, 66,* 410–427.

Berger, R. (1989, July). Promoting minority access to the profession. *Social Work,* 346-349.

Brissett-Chapman, S. (1994). Ethical dilemmas: A moral framework for leadership and decision making. *The Child and Youth Care Administrator, 6,* 23–25.

Cross, T. L., Bazron, B. J., Dennis, K. W., & Issacs, M. R. (1989, March). *Towards a culturally competent system of care, Volume I.* Washington, DC: CASSP Technical Assistance Center at Georgetown University Child Development Center.

Dore, M. M., Doris, J. M., & Wright, P. (1995, May). Identifying substance abuse in maltreating families: A child welfare challenge. *Child Abuse and Neglect, 19*, 531–543.

Edwards, E. D., & Edwards, M. E. (1995). Social work practice with American Indians and Alaskan Natives. In A. T. Morales & B. W. Shaefor (Eds.), *Social work: A profession of many faces.* Boston: Allyn and Bacon.

Ewalt, P. L., Freeman, E. M., Kirk, S. A., & Poole, D. L. (Eds.). (1996). *Multicultural issues in social work.* Washington, DC: NASW Press.

Finkelhor, D. (1993, January/February). Epidemiological factors in the clinical identification of child sexual abuse. *Child Abuse & Neglect, 17*, 67–70.

Gilles, T., & Kroll, J. (1991, April). *Barriers to same race placement.* St. Paul, MN: North American Council on Adoptable Children.

Jones, B. J. (1995). *The Indian Child Welfare Act handbook: A legal guide to the custody and adoption of Native American children.* Chicago: Section of Family Law Publications, American Bar Association.

Kallgren, C. A., & Caudill, P. J. (1993). Current transracial adoption practices: Racial dissonance or racial awareness? *Psychological Reports, 72*, 551–558.

Leung, P., Cheung, K.-F. M., & Stevenson, K. M. (1994, November/December). A strengths approach to ethnically sensitive practice for child protective service workers. *Child Welfare, 73*, 707–721.

Mann, J. T. (1994). Diversity: Professional and personal challenges for executive leadership. *Child and Youth Care Administrator, 6*, 20–22.

Manoleas, P. (1994). Social work: An outcome approach to assessing the cultural competence of MSW students. *Journal of Multicultural Social Work, 3*, 43–57.

National Association of Social Workers. (2001). *NASW standards for cultural competence in social work practice.* Washington, DC: NASW Press.

Pancost, R. (1994). Ten reasons for the increase in executive stress. *Child and Youth Care Administrator, 6*, 11–15.

Preli, R., & Bernard, J. M. (1993, January). Making multiculturalism relevant for majority culture graduate students. *Journal of Marital and Family Therapy, 19*, 5–16.

Stevenson, K., Cheung, K-F. M., & Leung, P. (1992, July/August). A new approach to training child protective service workers for ethnically sensitive practice. *Child Welfare, 71*, 291–303.

Sullivan, A. (1994). Update on transracial adoption. *Children's Voice, 3*, 4–6.

Race, Culture, and Ethnicity

Abernethy, A. D. (1995, April). Managing racial anger: A critical skill in cultural competence. *Journal of Multicultural Counseling and Development, 23*, 96–101.

Back, L., & Solomos, J. (Eds.). (2000). *Theories of race and racism: A reader*. New York: Routledge.

Courtney, M. E., Barth, R. P., Berrick, J. D., Brooks, D., Needell, B., & Park, L. (1996, March/April). Race and child welfare services: Past research and future directions. *Child Welfare, 75*, 99–137.

Dippie, B. W. (1982). *The vanishing American: White attitudes and U.S. Indian policy*. Lawrence, KS: University Press of Kansas.

Fadiman, A. (1997). *The spirit catches you and you fall down: A Hmong child, her American doctors and the collision of two cultures*. New York: Noonday Press.

Gordon, L. (1999). *The great Arizona orphan abduction*. Cambridge, MA: Harvard University Press.

Green, J. W. (1999). *Cultural awareness in the human services: A multi-ethnic approach*. Needham Heights, MA: Allyn and Bacon.

Katlin, F. (1982, March). The impact of ethnicity. *Social Casework, 63*, 168–171.

Kinder, D. R., & Mendelberg, T. (1995, May). Cracks in American apartheid: The political impact of prejudice among desegregated whites. *Journal of Politics, 57*, 402–424.

Long, C. (1999). Honoring diversity: The reliability, validity, and utility of a scale to measure cultural resiliency. *Journal of Human Behavior in the Social Environment, 2*(1).

McIntosh, P. (1989, July/August). White privilege: Unpacking the invisible knapsack. *Peace and Freedom*, 10–11.

Min, P. G., & Kim, R. (Eds.). (1999). *Struggle for ethnic identity: Narratives by Asian American professionals*. Walnut Creek, CA: Altamira Press.

Rodriguez, G. G. (1999). *Raising nuestros niños in a bicultural world*. New York: Fireside Books.

Tatum, B. D. (1997). *Why are all the black kids sitting together in the cafeteria? And other conversations about race*. New York: Basic Books.

Sexual Orientation

Mallon, G. P. (2001). *Lesbian and gay youth issues: A practical guide for youth workers*. Washington, DC: CWLA Press.

Morrow, D. F. (1993, November). Social work with gay and lesbian adolescents. *Social Work, 38*, 655–660.

O'Connell, A. (1993, June). Voices from the heart: The developmental impact of a mother's lesbianism on her adolescent children. *Smith College in Social Work, 63*, 281–299.

Rotheram-Borus, M. J., Rasario, M., Reid, H., & Koopman, C. (1995, April). Predicting patterns of sexual acts among homosexual and bisexual youth. *American Journal of Psychiatry, 152*, 588–594.

Tasker, F., & Golombok, S. (1995, April). Adults raised as children in lesbian families. *American Journal of Orthopsychiatry, 65*, 203–215.

For More Information

For more information about cultural competence, please contact

Jorge Velázquez Jr.
Director, Cultural Competence Division
Child Welfare League of America
50 F St., NW, Sixth Floor
Washington, DC 20001-1533
202/942-4906
E-mail: jvelazquez@cwla.org